ANIMALS NOBODY LOVES

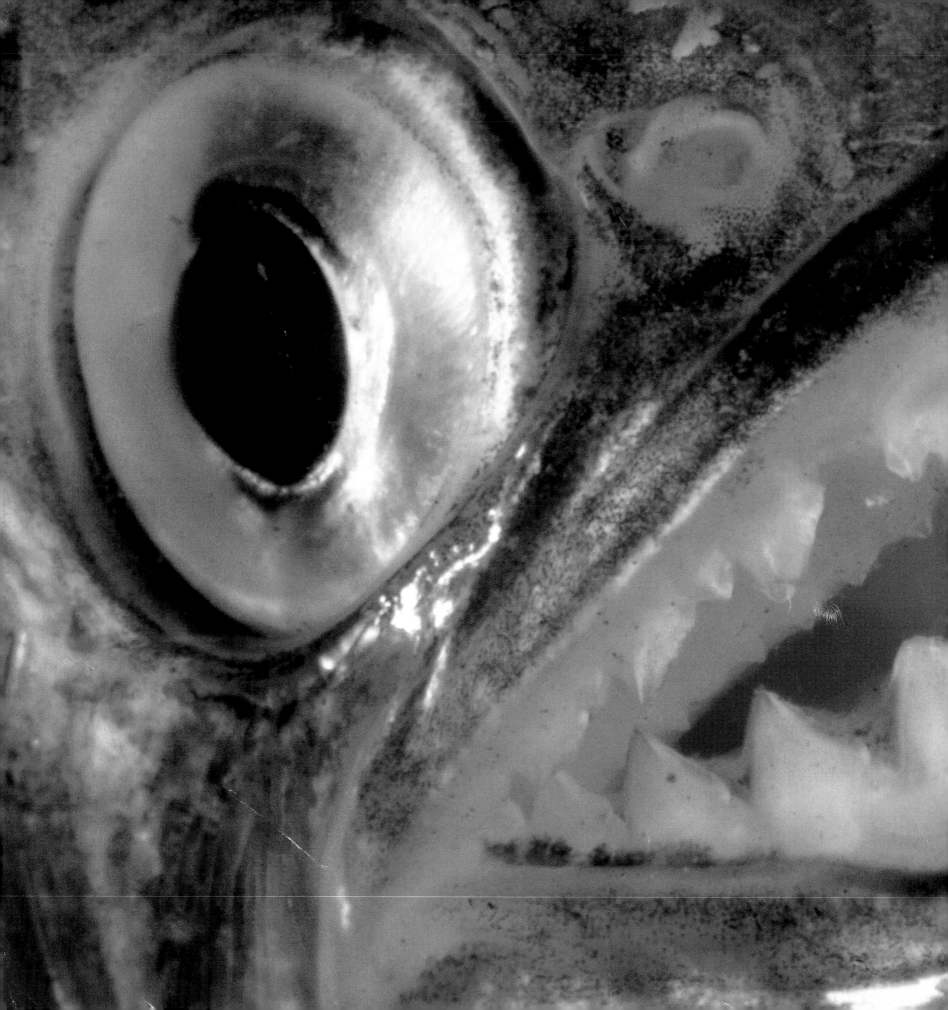

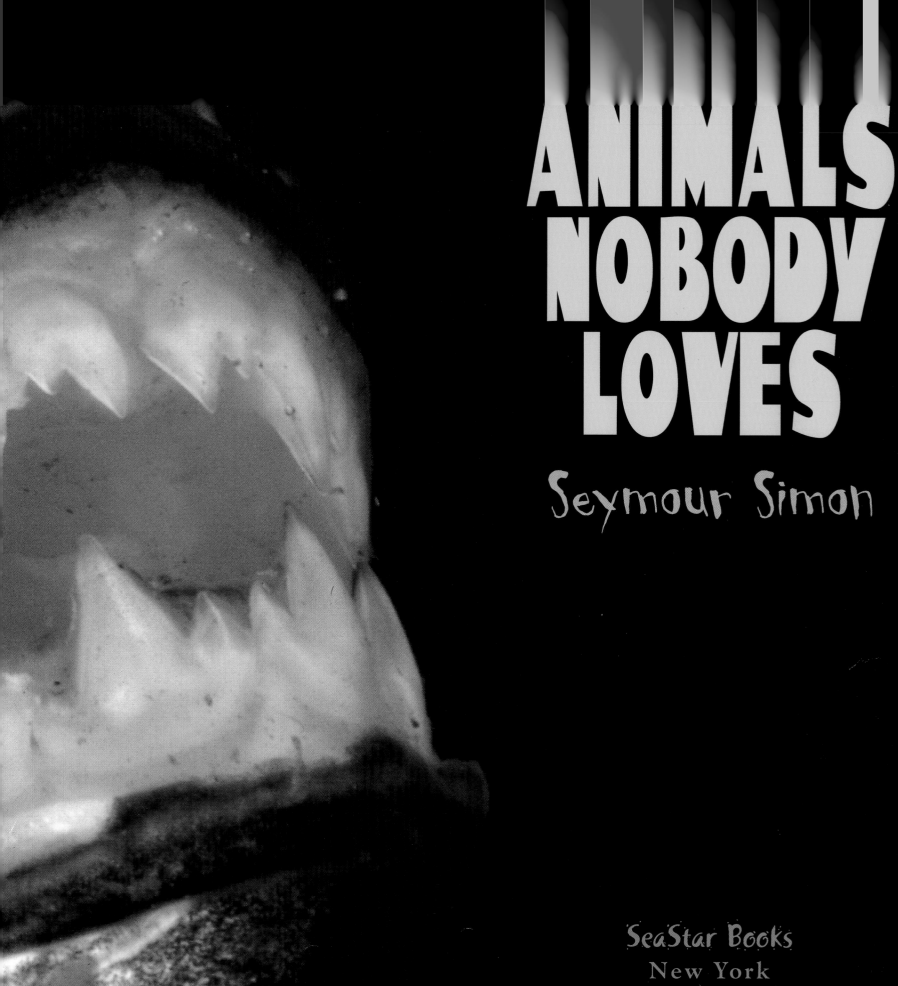

ANIMALS
NOBODY
LOVES

Seymour Simon

SeaStar Books

New York

Permission to use the following photographs is gratefully acknowledged:
Bill Beatty/Visuals Unlimited: front cover, page 48; Mark J. Thomas/Dembinsky Photo Assoc.: page 1; Dr. Paul A. Zahl/Photo Researchers, Inc.: pages 2–3; Joe McDonald/Visuals Unlimited: pages 5, 18–19; Barbara Gerlich/Visuals Unlimited: page 6; Al Giddings/Images Inc.: page 9; Stephen Dalton/Photo Researchers, Inc.: pages 10–11, 28–29; Renee Lynn/Photo Researchers, Inc.: pages 13, 34–35; Lynn M. Stone: pages 14–15, 16–17, 21, 26–27; Jesse Cancelmo/Dembinsky Photo Assoc.: pages 22–23; Tom McHugh/Photo Researchers, Inc.: pages 25, 30–31; Anup Shah/Dembinsky Photo Assoc.: pages 32–33; Dave B. Fleetham/Visuals Unlimited: page 36; Kjell B. Sandved/Visuals Unlimited: page 37; James Robinson/Photo Researchers, Inc.: pages 38–39; John Gerlach/ Dembinsky Photo Assoc.: pages 40–41; Norbert Wu/www.norbertwu.com: pages 42–43; Gary Meszaros/Dembinsky Photo Assoc.: pages 44–45; Tom Ulrich: pages 46–47; Thomas Gula/Visuals Unlimited: back cover; Tom McHugh/Photo Researchers, Inc.: back flap.

SeaStar Books
A division of North-South Books Inc.

Published in the United States by SeaStar Books,
a division of North-South Books Inc., New York.
Published simultaneously in Canada, Australia, and New Zealand by North-South Books,
an imprint of Nord-Süd Verlag AG, Gossau Zürich, Switzerland.
Library of Congress Cataloging-in-Publication Data
Simon, Seymour.
Animals nobody loves / Seymour Simon.
p.   cm.
Originally published: New York: Random House, © 1980.
1. Dangerous animals—Juvenile literature. 2. Animals—Miscellanea—Juvenile literature. [1. Animals—Miscellanea.]
I. Title.
QL100.S58 2001
591.6'5—dc21   00-10412

The text for this book is set in 16-point Goudy Catalogue MT.

ISBN 1-58717-079-5 (trade edition)
1 3 5 7 9 HC 10 8 6 4 2
ISBN 1-58717-080-9 (library edition)
1 3 5 7 9 LE 10 8 6 4 2
ISBN 1-58717-155-4 (paperback edition)
1 3 5 7 9 PB 10 8 6 4 2

Printed in Italy

For more information about our books, and the authors and artists who create them, visit our web site: www.northsouth.com

CONTENTS

INTRODUCTION

Did you know that one blow of a grizzly bear can crush the skull of an elk? That a small fish called a piranha can be more dangerous than a shark?

This book is about animals that few people like and nobody loves. Some of these animals are dangerous. Some are pests. Still others may seem strange because of their appearance.

Many of the animals in this book have had stories told about them or books written about them. But it's likely that not everything you've heard or read about these animals is true. Some animals just have bad reputations that are not based on fact. Animals are not bad or evil. They do what they must in order to survive.

You may never love a rattlesnake, a cockroach, or an octopus—but this book may help you begin to understand and respect them for what they are.

SHARK

The shark is the most feared animal in the sea. Some sharks are large and dangerous. Others are just a few feet long and eat small fish. Sharks come in many different sizes, shapes, and colors. Hammerheads, tiger sharks, and mako sharks have powerful jaws and razor-sharp teeth. Some sharks can bite three hundred times harder than a human.

The most dangerous shark is the great white shark. It usually swims in the open sea. But sometimes a great white shark may attack and kill swimmers with no warning. It may even attack small boats. Its large, saw-edged teeth can rip through wood and even metal. The great white shark has a huge appetite and will eat any animal or person that it finds in its path.

BAT

Bats look like mice with wings. They look like birds, too, but they are not. Bats' wings have no feathers—they are covered with skin.

Some people think bats are blind because they fly back and forth so strangely. But bats are not blind. Bats can see, and they give off high-pitched sounds that echo back from objects to their ears. That helps the bats to navigate even in total darkness.

Some kinds of bats eat fruit. There are also bats that catch small animals such as mice, bats that can catch small fish, and vampire bats, which suck blood from animals such as cattle.

People have many strange ideas about bats. Bats do not attack people. They do not get stuck in people's hair. In fact, most bats can be helpful to us, because they eat insect pests such as mosquitoes.

GRIZZLY BEAR

A large grizzly bear is one of the strongest animals in the world. A full-grown male is over eight feet long from nose to tail and can weigh more than seven hundred pounds. Grizzlies eat everything from squirrels to deer, and from berries to birds. Almost any animal in grizzly country may wind up as a meal for this mighty hunter.

Once, the grizzly was the most feared animal of the American Northwest. Many thousands of grizzlies lived all along the Pacific Coast. But now only a few hundred grizzlies are left. Even the grizzly was no match for a bullet from a high-powered rifle, or the loss of its hunting lands to people turning the range into farms and ranches.

There is no doubt that a grizzly bear is a dangerous animal and should be left alone. Any encounter with a bear can be frightening. If you see a bear that is far away or doesn't see you, turn around and go back. If the bear is close or does see you, remain calm. *Do not run*. Instead, stand tall or back away slowly and wave your hands and speak loudly. The chances are that the bear will not bother you and will disappear.

COBRA

This Indian cobra is only about five and a half feet long, one-third the size of the largest poisonous snake in the world, the king cobra. Since Indian cobras are commonly found in populated areas and often go into houses to catch rats, they are the ones that most often bite people.

The fangs in the front of a cobra's mouth inject a deadly poison that can paralyze a person or an animal. In about one of ten cases, cobra bites are fatal. In India alone, cobras are reported to kill thousands of people each year, more than sharks all over the world do in fifty years.

When threatened, a cobra spreads its hood by raising and pushing forward the long ribs behind its neck. The skin stretches across the ribs, forming a hood that may be four times as wide as the snake's body. Few sights are more terrifying than a fifteen-foot-long king cobra, its hood erect, preparing to strike!

VULTURE

Most people don't like vultures because they eat dead animals. The sight of vultures circling in the sky is a sign that an animal is near death. When the animal dies, vultures land and cluster in a group around the body, tearing at the flesh.

There are different kinds of vultures all over the world. Vultures are big birds, and some can spread their wings to twelve feet. Vultures' heads are naked or covered by only a few feathers. They have hooked beaks like hawks and eagles. Vultures may be related to hawks and eagles, but they aren't nearly as popular. In fact, most people think vultures' looks and habits are downright repulsive.

Vultures may be ugly, but they fly beautifully. Vultures soar high on air currents in the daytime. They use their powerful eyesight to find food. They can sometimes spot a dying animal forty miles away.

SPIDER

Many people think spiders are horrible creatures. They are afraid that spiders will jump up and bite them. Some people run away when they see a spider. Others try to kill any spider they see.

But spiders do not normally bite human beings. Spiders usually trap insects they prey upon—from flies and mosquitoes to grasshoppers and crickets—in beautiful silken webs. Then they bite the insect and inject a poison to quiet it down so that they can eat it. So we should remember that spiders do us a lot of good by getting rid of insect pests.

Of course, if you trap a spider and try to grab it, it may bite you. The bite of most spiders is harmless. But a few spiders, such as the black widow, are very poisonous. A bite from a black widow can make people sick or even kill them. It's a good idea just to watch spiders and not bother them.

HYENA

The hyena looks like a large dog. Its front legs are longer than its back ones, so its body slopes downward. Another name for the hyena is the laughing hyena. Hyenas roam in packs on the plains of Africa. During the night, hyenas howl. When they come near their prey, they make noises that sound like crazy laughter.

The hyena has a good sense of smell that helps it find food. Like the vulture, the hyena eats dead and dying animals. It arrives after the vultures have feasted. The hyena uses its powerful jaws and teeth to crush the bones left over by lions, cheetahs, and leopards.

Hyenas also attack old or injured animals. But when a dangerous animal such as a lion attacks a hyena, it rarely tries to defend itself. First it tries to escape. Then the hyena plays dead until it gets the chance to run away.

—

DEVIL RAY

The giant devil ray can measure more than twenty feet across. With their long whiplike tails and a pair of "horns" just in front of their eyes, perhaps it is their strange appearance and great size that made people fear them and call them devil rays. But this name gives the wrong idea about these peaceful animals. A devil ray is very powerful but doesn't deliberately attack people. However, if harpooned, a devil ray may turn over a boat while attempting to escape. Unlike the stingray, its cousin, the devil ray does not have a stinging spine on its tail.

Devil rays swim slowly and gracefully through warm ocean waters, flapping their great triangular "wings." They usually swim at or near the surface, at times leaping out of the water, and sometimes lying quietly in the sun. Devil rays feed on fish and other small water animals that they sweep into their mouths with their "horns."

RATTLESNAKE

A rattlesnake is a poisonous snake that has a rattle at the end of its tail. When a rattlesnake is alarmed, it coils its body, lifting its head and tail off the ground. The tail moves back and forth so the rattles make a buzzing sound. The rattle is not used when the rattlesnake is hunting. The noise would scare away the snake's meal. The snake only uses its rattle to warn away animals or humans that may be harmful to it.

A rattlesnake bites with its hollow teeth, called fangs. It pumps poison through its fangs into the victim. The snake then feeds on rats, mice, toads, and frogs by unhinging its jaws and swallowing its meal whole.

There are at least twenty-eight different kinds of rattlesnakes. The eastern diamondback rattler, found in the eastern United States, is the largest. It may grow to over six feet long and weigh more than thirty pounds.

GILA MONSTER

The Gila (pronounced HEE-la) is called a monster because of its terrible poisonous bite, not its size. The Gila monster is a lizard less than two feet long. It is the only poisonous lizard in the United States. The bite of a Gila monster is just as dangerous as that of a rattlesnake.

The black-and-yellow Gila moves slowly along the desert sands looking for birds' eggs to eat. It also feeds on rabbits and other small animals. The Gila doesn't use poison to kill small prey. Its bite is strong enough to kill.

If a person bothers a Gila, it turns and snaps with lightning speed. When the Gila bites, its jaws clamp down hard. It sinks its teeth deep into the person and holds on like a bulldog. Poison slowly flows through its mouth and into the victim. Few people are bitten by Gila monsters—only those foolish enough to try to handle one.

RAT

The rat is the animal that many people dislike the most. Unlike sharks and grizzlies and many of the other animals in this book, rats are everywhere. No place is free from rats except for the coldest spots on Earth, such as Antarctica, the northern Arctic, and the tops of ice-covered mountains. Experts say that there are more rats than people living in the United States.

The rat is a small, furry rodent. It has sharp teeth that can gnaw through wood and metal. Rats eat any food that people eat. They live in garbage dumps and slums and also in expensive houses. Wherever they go, they spoil food and spread dirt and disease. People are always at war with rats.

The bubonic plague, or "Black Death," was spread by flea-infested rats during the 1300s. More than 25 million deaths were caused by this disease—one-third of the entire population of Europe at that time.

COCKROACH

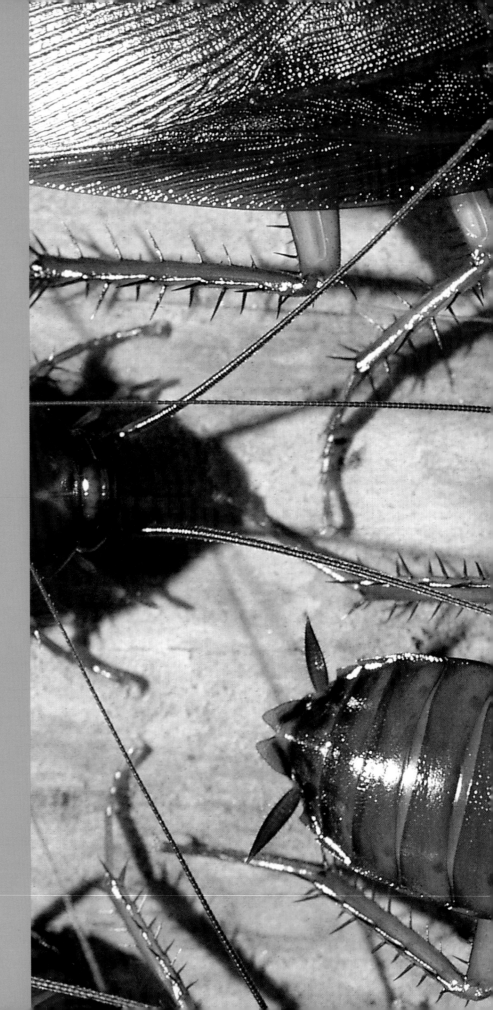

Cockroaches are insects that have lived on the Earth for more than 200 million years—far longer than humans. Like rats, cockroaches are found all over the world except in the coldest places.

There are many kinds of cockroaches. Some of the biggest ones are about as long as your little finger. The largest cockroaches in the world are found in the tropics and can be more than three inches long and a half-inch wide.

Cockroaches are very hardy insects. A headless cockroach can live for as long as a week. Roaches can run as fast as three miles an hour, and a young roach can fit through a crack as thin as a dime.

Cockroaches like the dark, so when you turn on the light in a roach-infested kitchen, they scurry off in all directions. Cockroaches also like damp spots under sinks or near drains. They come out at night to look for crumbs or any food left around the house. It's even harder to get rid of cockroaches than rats.

CROCODILE

Crocodiles are large lizards that live in rivers, lakes, and bays. Some crocodiles are twenty-five feet long. Crocodiles are very dangerous. They will go after humans without any fear.

Most crocodiles hunt for prey too large to be swallowed at a single gulp. Crocs can't chew, so they have to tear their prey apart by grasping an arm or a leg and thrashing their bodies around. Sometimes they drown their victims and sometimes they do not.

SKUNK

The skunk has two white stripes on its back. The stripes tell you to watch out!

If you don't bother a skunk, it won't bother you. But if a skunk gets angry or frightened, it can spray a bad-smelling liquid as far as ten feet. The skunk turns around and raises its tail when danger comes near. If that doesn't scare away the enemy, the skunk uses its spray. There is enough for six shots in a row, but one blast is usually enough. A direct hit on an animal or person causes burning in the eyes, nose, or mouth. If the spray gets on clothes, the smell can last for weeks. Even your best friend won't come near you when you smell like a skunk.

A skunk is usually peaceful. It walks along slowly, looking for insects to eat. It also likes berries, fruits, and seeds. People don't often see a skunk because it goes out mostly at night.

MAN-of-WAR

The man-of-war is frequently mistaken for a jellyfish. Sometimes called the Portuguese man-of-war, it is often seen in warm ocean and coastal waters. However, the man-of-war is not a single animal but a colony of different kinds of creatures that coexist. The blue six-inch balloon, or float, keeps the colony on the surface. Streaming down from the float are hundreds of thin stinging tentacles. Some tentacles are short, while others may reach a length of forty feet or more.

In just one tentacle, there are thousands of stingers that can hurt people as badly as the stings of a huge swarm of bees or wasps. The stings can cause fever, shock, and circulatory and respiratory problems. The man-of-war catches small fish, shrimps, and other sea animals by stinging and then digesting them.

Men-of-war are carried by ocean currents and are often washed ashore. But even after a man-of-war is dead, the tentacles may still sting people who pick them up or stumble upon them in the sand.

FIRE ANT

Fire ants look like ordinary ants that you may find in your house or garden. They are called fire ants because their bites and stings are painful and burn like fire. The most dangerous kind are red fire ants. These are small reddish or dark brown ants, only about one-quarter-inch long.

Fire ants have a poison that can paralyze insects, earthworms, and other small animals. Squirrels, chickens, pigs, and even calves have died as a result of being stung.

Fire ants nesting around homes, in school yards, and in parks can be dangerous to young children and pets. A fire-ant nest is sometimes three feet high and nearly two feet across. More than one hundred thousand fire ants may live in a single mound. Fire ants are found across the southeastern United States and Texas.

COYOTE

When the sun goes down, the coyote leaves its den and begins its serenade. It howls, barks, whines, and yaps. These sounds carry for miles around in the still night air. One lone coyote can sound like a whole pack!

The coyote looks like a medium-size dog with a bushy tail. There are some reports of coyotes attacking pet dogs and cats and—very rarely—young children. But most coyotes steer clear of people, even though you may hear them singing their songs at night across the Northeast, South, and Midwest as well as in the western states.

Many sheep ranchers hunt coyotes because they think coyotes kill a lot of their animals. But coyotes do not kill many sheep. More often, they kill rabbits and mice that eat the grass that sheep need. So the coyote really does more good than harm to the sheep rancher.

OCTOPUS

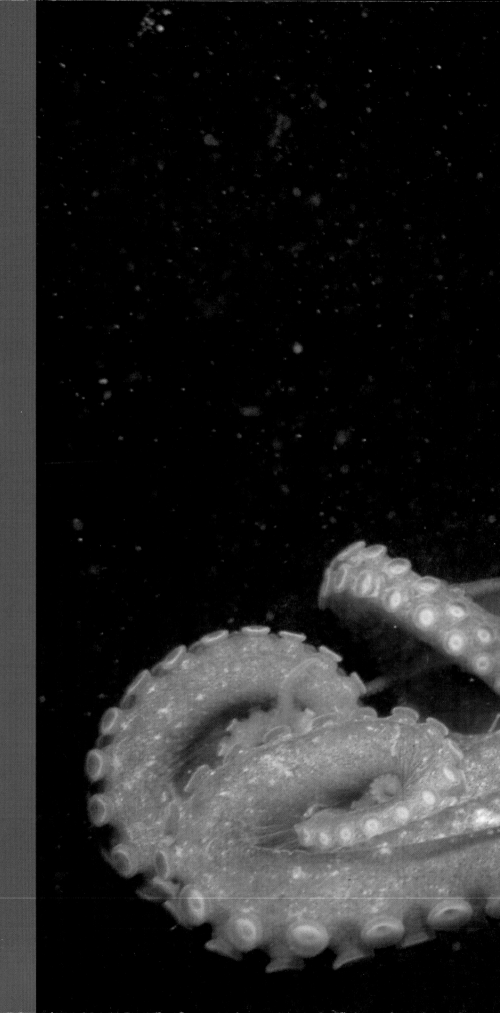

An octopus is a sea animal that seems to be all head and arms. The eight arms, or tentacles, are long and each one has two rows of suction disks that can hold tightly to almost anything.

Octopuses live in the cracks between underwater rocks. Most octopuses are only about two or three feet long—but the largest ones may be as much as thirty feet across. An octopus eats crabs and lobsters, seizing them with its arms and breaking their shells with its sharp jaws.

Some people think of an octopus as a terrible monster that attacks any diver swimming near its cave. But the octopus is really shy and harmless. It will never bite humans unless they are trying to capture it. Usually an octopus will spray a cloud of dark inky fluid and try to escape instead of fighting back.

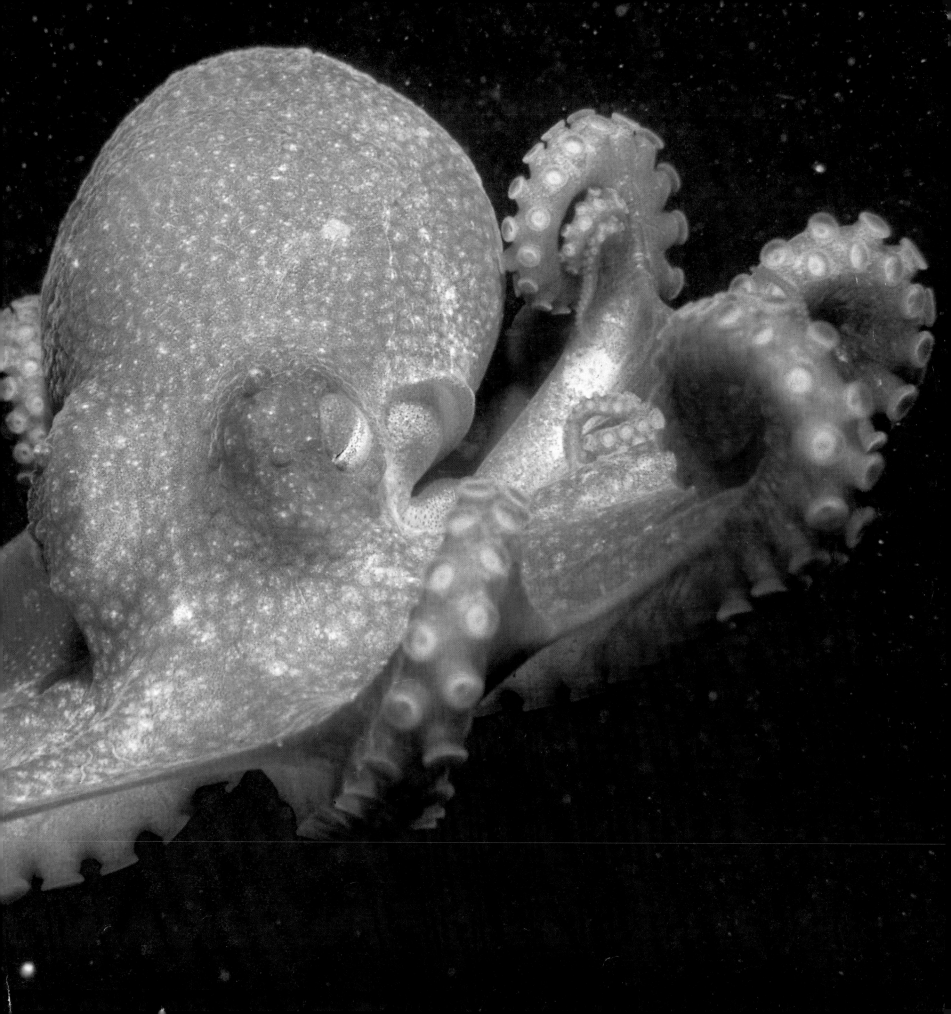

WASP

Wasps are stinging insects. Some kinds of wasp are also called yellow jackets, and other kinds are called hornets.

Yellow jackets are often uninvited guests at outdoor picnics. They crawl over peanut-butter-and-jelly sandwiches, and land on people in their search for sugary foods. They usually will not sting unless they are bothered. Yellow jackets are most dangerous when their nests are disturbed, swarming forth in clouds of stinging fury at an intruder. A single yellow jacket can sting more than once.

Wasps build paper nests in trees or bushes, in buildings and outdoor furniture, in stumps, and in caves. The paper is made of chewed plant material mixed with wasp saliva. A nest is started in the spring by a single queen and grows to the size of a football by autumn, when it contains hundreds or even thousands of wasps. Except for a few queens who hibernate in sheltered places, the entire colony of wasps dies in the first severe frost.

PIRANHA

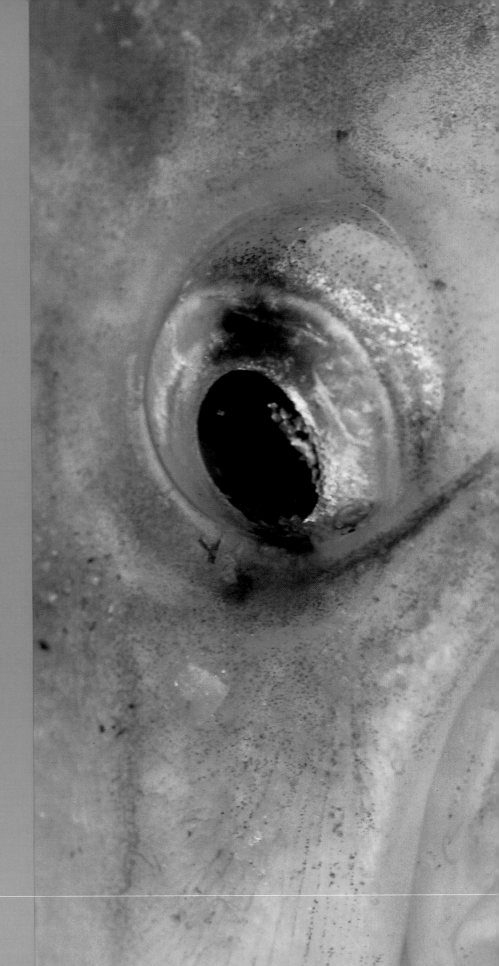

The piranha is a freshwater fish less than one foot long. It is smaller than the smallest shark. Despite its size, the piranha is often called the most dangerous fish in the world. Piranhas have killed more people than the great white shark!

A piranha's broad jaws have a row of razor-sharp teeth. When the piranha closes its jaws, its teeth lock together tightly. One bite can slice through bone in an instant.

Large numbers of piranhas live in streams and rivers in the forests of South America. They gather together wherever there is food. If an animal wanders into the water, it is attacked by a swarm of piranhas. The fish go into a frenzy at the smell of blood, biting out in all directions.

Piranhas can strip the flesh from a large animal in just a few minutes. There are horrible stories of people being eaten alive by piranhas. No wonder this small fish is so feared.

Do you feel any differently about the animals in this book now that you know more about them? If you do, can you think of the reasons that made you change your mind? Perhaps you might make your own list of animals that *you* don't love and think about why each of these animals is on your list.